All About

HORSES

Everything A
✿ HORSE-CRAZY GIRL
Needs to Know

by Molly Kolpin

Consultant:
C. Michael Kerns, DVM
Director of Veterinary Services
The University of Findlay
Findlay, Ohio

CAPSTONE PRESS
a capstone imprint

Snap Books are published by Capstone Press,
1710 Roe Crest Drive, North Mankato, Minnesota 56003
www.capstonepub.com

Library of Congress Cataloging-in-Publication Data
Kolpin, Molly
All about horses : everything a horse-crazy girl needs to know
/ by Molly Kolpin.
pages cm. — (Snap books. Crazy about horses)
Summary: "Text and photos introduce readers to general
information about horses, including physical characteristics,
historical origin, life cycle, body language, and horses in
pop culture"— Provided by publisher.
Audience: Ages 8–14.
Audience: Grades 4 to 6.
Includes bibliographical references and index.
ISBN 978-1-4914-0710-3 (library binding)
ISBN 978-1-4914-0716-5 (eBook PDF)
1. Horses—Juvenile literature. 2. Horses—Behavior—Juvenile
literature. 3. Horses—Life cycles—Juvenile literature. I. Title.
SF302.K65 2015
636.1—dc23   2014002750

Editorial Credits
Michelle Hasselius, editor; Juliette Peters, designer;
Deirdre Barton, media researcher,
Laura Manthe, production specialist

Photo Credits
Capstone Studio: Karon Dubke: 28, 29 (bottom); Center for
American History, UT Austin: Heinrick Harder Art: 7 (top);
Corbis: Bettman: 24; Newscom: Florilegius: 6; Shutterstock:
Abramova Kseniya: cover, 10, 31, Anakondasp: 12, 17 (top
middle), Anastasilia Golovokova: 3 (bottom right), 5 (b), 30,
Anastasija Popova: 9 (b), 11 (bl), Ashkabe: 17 (tr), Bine: 26,
BMJ: 12 (tr), Cheryl Ann Quigley: 21 (b), Christian Mueller:
18, Claudia Steininger: 15 (b), DaCek: 13 (bl), Defotoberg:
22, Eastern Light Photography: 17 (tl), Ekina: 19 (bm), Eric
Isselee: 7 (b), 9 (t), Goran Bogicevic: 4, Jklingebiel: 2–3, Kotenko
Oleksandr: 32, Lenkadan: 13 (mr), Lorelei Girod-b: 19 (tr),
Makarova Vikoria: 11 (tr), 17 (b), Mariait: 8, 13 (ml), 19 (tm, bl),
27 (b), 14, Myway8: 13 (tl), Nicole Ciscato: 16, 19 (br), Reddogs:
25, Stefan Holm, 5 (r), StudioNewmarket: 29 (t), Tamara
Didenko: 1, Theunis Jacobus Botha: 21 (t), Thirteen: 11 (b),
Tom Plesnik: 23, Vespa: 27 (t), Viktori Makarva Zh) e
20, Zuzule: 11 (tl), 15 (t), 19 (tl); Wikipedia: Horse and a
Woman by Theodore Hoe Mead, 5).

All design elements are credited to Shutterstock.

Glossary terms are bolded on first use in text.

Printed in the United States of America in North Mankato, Minnesota.
072018   000810

TABLE of CONTENTS

Horses RULE. Dogs DROOL!

If a dog is man's best friend, then for girls this honor goes to the horse. With their large, intelligent eyes and curious, loyal natures, horses ma[...] companions. Sure a ho[...]

A rider who sits **sidesaddle** has both legs on one side of the horse.

DID YOU KNOW?

For many centuries it was considered unladylike for girls to sit **astride** a horse. Instead they had to ride sidesaddle.

SAFETY FIRST!

Never approach a horse without permission or adult supervision. Not all of these animals are gentle giants!

A Gallop through History

Sixty million years ago, horses began to develop in the southeastern area of North America. The horse's earliest **ancestors** were little larger than rabbits. They ran on feet with toes and filled their bellies with leaves. They looked a bit like small foxes with long necks.

Slowly these animals spread to other continents and transformed into modern-day horses. Their toed feet turned into hooves, and they began to eat grass instead of leaves. Most noticeably their size grew until they became the big, powerful animals you know today.

The dawn h

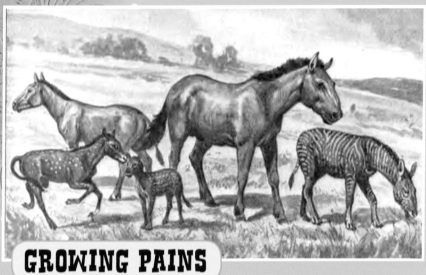

GROWING PAINS

The horse's transformation over time was filled with twists and turns. It wasn't a tidy, straightforward process. Many strange-looking animals separate today's horse from its earliest ancestors.

DID YOU KNOW?

Horses are part of the scientific group called Equus. This group also includes zebras and donkeys.

TIP *to* TAIL

Horses' flowing manes and shiny coats have won over countless admirers. But their looks have more to do with practicality than prettiness. When living in the wild, horses needed to be able to outrun dangerous **predators**, such as wolves and mountain lions. They developed strong, muscular legs to help them sprint. Narrow faces and bodies reduce wind resistance and help horses maintain high speeds when galloping.

Not every feature on a horse was designed for speed, however. A horse's long neck lets it graze for grass. Its swishy tail helps it swat at pesky flies. All these practical qualities result in a gorgeous animal!

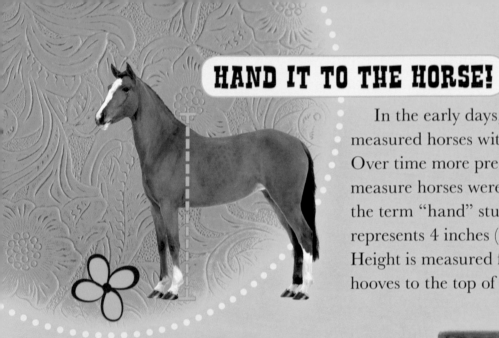

HAND IT TO THE HORSE!

In the early days, people measured horses with their hands. Over time more precise ways to measure horses were developed, but the term "hand" stuck. One hand represents 4 inches (10 centimeters). Height is measured from a horse's hooves to the top of its **withers**.

DID YOU KNOW?

Horses can lock their rear legs in place, which allows them to sleep while standing.

Coat Colors

When most girls think of horses, the colors black or brown come to mind. But horse coats actually include a wide variety of colors. Dapple gray, for example, is a gray coat with darker-colored rings. A gray coat with brown flecks is called fleabitten. Strawberry-roan is chestnut and white, while blue roan is black or brown with white. Bay refers to a horse with a solid-colored coat and a black mane, tail, and legs.

The list goes on and on. Add spots and patches to the mix, and it's easy to see why horse coloring is a complicated topic!

bay

COMMON FACIAL MARKINGS

bald face

blaze

star

snip

Sensible Steeds

Like people, horses experience the world through their five senses. Large eyes on the sides of their heads allow horses to see in almost all directions. On a windy day, horses can take in scents from up to 1 mile (1.6 kilometers) away. Horses also pick up on sounds carried by the wind. They twist their ears in all directions to pinpoint noises.

Because horses have taste buds, their sense of taste is very similar to humans. But this animal has a special trick when it comes to touch. Not only do horses feel through their skin, but they also feel through extra-sensitive whiskers on their **muzzles**.

DID YOU KNOW?

Horses have larger eyes than any other land mammal.

HORSE VS. HUMAN

Horses have the same five senses you do,
but they use their senses differently.

1. Horses can see _____
colors than humans.
a. more   **b.** fewer

4. Unlike humans, horses have
a special body part called the
_____ that helps them smell.
a. nostril aid   **b.** scent detector
c. Jacobson's organ

2. Horses can hear _____ noises
that humans can't.
a. low-pitched   **b.** high-pitched
c. faraway   **d.** all of the above

3. Both horses and humans
can taste _____.
a. sweet   **b.** salty
c. sour   **d.** bitter
e. all of the above

5. Horses have tough skin,
but they're sensitive to
touch like humans thanks
to countless _____.
a. nerve endings
b. feeler fingers
c. touch entrappers

Answer Key:
1.b 2.d 3.e 4.c 5.a

A Neighborly CHAT

Horses communicate with each other through their own special language. Humans have no way of knowing for sure how horse-speak translates into language. But careful observations have led to some pretty good guesses.

When a horse neighs, it's usually checking in with another horse or greeting its owner. Sometimes horses make rumbling sounds called nickers. This can be interpreted as a friendly hello. Watch out for the not-so-friendly roar. A horse that makes this sound is usually angry!

GIRL POWER!

Wild horse herds have their own leader system. A male is in charge of protecting the herd. But the herd's decision-maker is a female. This older female is in charge of locating food, water, and shelter for the group. She also disciplines the younger horses and even leads the herd when running from predators.

DID YOU KNOW?

"Whinny" is another term for "neigh."

Equine Signs

Horses don't always use noises to communicate. In fact most of their communication happens through **body language**. They use their ears, eyes, hooves, and tails to show how they're feeling.

A horse perks up its ears and points them forward when it's alert and ready to go. When it's angry, it will pin its ears back flat against its head. If a horse is relaxed, chances are its tail will be relaxed. But if a horse is crabby, its tail will be stiff or switching back and forth. A horse that stamps its hooves is probably cranky. Be especially careful if a horse is stamping its hooves with wide eyes and flared nostrils. This could be a sign the horse is ready to kick!

KEEP YOUR EYES ON THE EARS!

Read a horse's mood at a glance by memorizing these common ear signals.

alert

ears are up and
face forward

relaxed or sleepy

ears
point sideways

angry

ears are
pinned back

DID YOU KNOW?

Sometimes horses communicate
by rearing up on their hind legs.
This action is usually done to
scare an enemy.

EARLY Days

Newborn horses called foals are usually born in the spring. A foal's size can vary, depending on the **breed**. The foal stands up on its long, thin legs within its first hour of life. Before a day passes, it can both walk and run.

Just because a foal moves like an adult horse doesn't mean it looks like one. Instead of smooth, shiny coats, foals are covered in soft, fluffy coats. Their legs are long for their bodies. They have short tails and thin, wispy manes that stick straight up. It takes about four months before foals start to look like adults. At 6 months old, a foal is ready to leave its mother and live life on its own.

DID YOU KNOW?

Horses can live to be 25 years old or older.

A HORSE'S LIFE

foal—a young horse (under 1 year old) that drinks its mother's milk

weanling—a young horse (about 6 months to 1 year of age) that has stopped drinking its mother's milk

yearling—a horse between 1 and 2 years old

filly—a female horse that's less than 4 years old
colt—a male horse that's less than 4 years old

mare—a female horse that's at least 4 years old

stallion—a male horse that's at least 4 years old and can be used for breeding

Learning the Ropes

Horses are adults when they're 4 years old. But horses that will carry riders have a lot to learn before reaching adulthood. First they must get used to people. Good trainers will start handling young horses right away. The trainer should have positive interactions with the horse so it bonds with humans. For example, safely handling a horse's hoof can build trust. Through positive and safe interactions, horses can learn to be calm around people. These processes are called gentling. Gentling can take a year or more, depending on the horse.

Horses should be introduced to riding equipment when they are yearlings. By the age of 2 or 3, most horses are ready to carry their first riders. Only experienced riders should handle young horses.

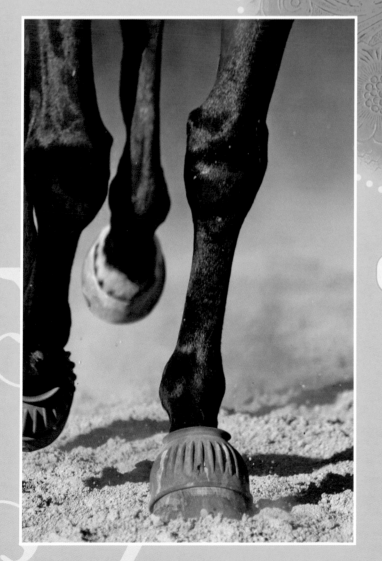

TRAINING LEGS

A horse's legs aren't fully developed until it's 1 or 2 years old. If a horse is exercised for too long before it reaches this age, it may become injured. Make sure a horse can safely carry a person's weight before riding it.

DID YOU KNOW?

Some racehorses begin their careers at just 2 years old.

HORSES
Then AND *Now*

Horses and humans have worked as teams for thousands of years. Originally horses were used to herd sheep and cattle. But people quickly realized horses could help them in other ways as well. They used horses as a means of transportation and also to carry warriors into battle.

Today vehicles and machines have replaced many of the horse's traditional jobs. But in North America and Australia, some horses are still used to herd livestock. Cowboys in the western United States, for in t n e e t n o a le A teady horse will o o u y n e on oping the animal. Horse a a t t ul through thick forests where v h es '

A HORSE ON THE FORCE!

One of the modern-day horse's most important jobs is to help the police. Big-city police forces use horses to carry officers through crowded streets. Officers on horseback have a better view of crowds than they do on foot.

DID YOU KNOW?

Humans first started working with horses around 5,000 years ago.

Horse Hobbies

Though horses have fewer jobs than in the past, they remain as popular as ever. Instead of putting horses to work, people now use them for recreation. Horse competitions such as show jumping and **dressage** have become popular in recent years.

Horse enthusiasts especially love watching racehorses sprint around a track. Famous races such as the Kentucky Derby draw millions of viewers each year. Some horses have even become famous entertainers, such as Bamboo Harvester. Bamboo Harvester played the talking horse on the 1960s' TV show *Mister Ed*. Horses have even starred in popular films such as *Secretariat* and *Dreamer*.

Bamboo Harvester starred in *Mister Ed* from 1961 until 1966.

DID YOU KNOW?

Secretariat was the winner of the Kentucky Derby in 1973. He crossed the finish line at the record-breaking time of 1:59 2/5 minutes.

ARE YOU HORSE OBSESSED?

1. Your favorite shoes to shop for are:
   a. riding boots
   b. sneakers
   c. sandals

2. Your ideal vacation would take place:
   a. at a horse ranch
   b. on a tropical island
   c. in a big city

3. When you grow up, you want to be:
   a. a riding instructor
   b. a doctor
   c. a fashion designer

4. At the library, you most often check out books from this series:
   a. *The Saddle Club* by Bonnie Bryant
   b. *The Baby-Sitters Club* by Ann M. Martin
   c. *Harry Potter* by J.K. Rowling

5. You would wait in line for hours to get tickets to:
   a. the Kentucky Derby
   b. a Justin Bieber concert
   c. a movie premiere

6. Your favorite sport to watch is:
   a. polo
   b. gymnastics
   c. tennis

7. You know that jodhpurs are:
   a. riding pants
   b. handheld electronic gadgets
   c. tiny bugs that look like miniature butterflies

8. Your favorite way to spend a Saturday would be:
   a. horseback riding
   b. shopping
   c. painting

If all of your answers are "a," you're officially horse obsessed!

Giddy Up!

Few horse lovers can resist an opportunity to hop in the saddle and explore a trail. But hold your horses! Before riding into the sunset, it's important to learn about riding equipment.

To stay comfortable riders sit on a saddle and put their feet through stirrups. A rider uses reins to tell the horse where to go. Reins are attached to a bit, which goes in the horse's mouth. When a rider moves the reins, pressure is put on the bit. This tells the horse to turn or slow down. Horses should also wear horseshoes to protect their hooves from rough roads or trails.

RIDING RULES

A rider should always wear boots and a protective helmet. Boots should have heels so feet won't slip through the stirrups. (If a rider falls and gets a foot stuck in the stirrup, he or she could be dragged and badly injured.) Also make sure the helmet is meant for horseback riding. Bike helmets aren't designed to protect riders from horse accidents.

DID YOU KNOW?

Horses have four different **gaits**. From slowest to fastest, they are—walk, trot, canter, and gallop.

trot

Big Jobs. Big Rewards.

Owning a horse isn't all about adventurous trail rides or glamorous competitions in the show ring. Caring for a horse is a huge responsibility. Owners must make sure their horses are well fed and cared for. Horses need to be groomed, especially before and after riding. And they need at least 30 to 60 minutes of exercise several days a week. Owners must also muck out their horses' **stalls** every day. This involves work clearing out any dirty straw and manure.

Horse chores aren't always fun. But horse owners know these chores are a small price to pay for all the love they're offered in return. Give your heart to a horse, and you'll have a friend for life.

NO HORSE? NO PROBLEM.

Satisfy your horse obsession by:
- Joining an organization, such as 4-H
- Volunteering at a stable, zoo, or farm
- Reading books such as *The Saddle Club* by Bonnie Bryant or *The Thoroughbred* series by Joanna Campbell
- Watching horse movies, such as *Black Beauty* and *Secretariat*

DID YOU KNOW?

Horses eat about 15 to 20 pounds (7 to 9 kilograms) of hay per day.

GLOSSARY

ancestor (AN-sess-tur)—a member of a family who lived a long time ago

astride (uh-STRAHYD)—to ride with one leg on each side of a horse

body language (BAH-dee LANG-gwij)—the movements animals make to communicate with each other

breed (BREED)—a certain kind of animal within an animal group; breed also means to join together to produce young

dressage (dre-SAHZH)—an equestrian sport in which a trained horse shows its ability to move precisely and gracefully based on cues from its rider

gait (GATE)—the manner in which horses move; gaits include the walk, trot, canter, and gallop

muzzle (MUHZ-uhl)—the jaws, mouth, and nose of a horse

predator (PRED-uh-tur)—an animal that hunts other animals for food

sidesaddle (SAHYD-sad-uhl)—a riding position with both legs on the same side of a horse

stall (STAWL)—a compartment in a stable that houses a horse

withers (WITH-ers)— the high part of the back, at the base of a horse's neck

READ MORE

Wilsdon, Christina. *For Horse-Crazy Girls Only: Everything You Want to Know About Horses.* New York: Feiwel and Friends, 2010.

Woodward, John. *Horses: The Ultimate Treasury.* New York: DK Publishing, 2012.

Young, Rae. *The Ultimate Guide to Drawing Horses.* North Mankato, Minn.: Capstone Press, 2014.

INTERNET SITES

FactHound offers a safe, fun way to find Internet sites related to this book. All of the sites on FactHound have been researched by our staff.

Here's all you do:

Visit *www.facthound.com*

Type in this code: 9781491407103

 Check out projects, games and lots more at **www.capstonekids.com**

INDEX